Let Freedom Ring

The Salem Witch Trials

by Tracey Boraas

Consultant:
Walter W. Woodward
Assistant Professor of History
Dickinson College
Carlisle, Pennsylvania

Capstone
press

Mankato, Minnesota

Capstone Press
151 Good Counsel Drive, P.O. Box 669, Mankato, Minnesota 56002
www.capstonepress.com

Library of Congress Cataloging-in-Publication Data
Boraas, Tracey.
    The Salem witch trials / by Tracey Boraas.
       p. cm.—(Let freedom ring)
    Summary: Follows the beginnings of the witchcraft hysteria that led to the Salem
witch trials and describes the impact of these trials on the people and community.
    Includes bibliographical references and index.
    ISBN 0–7368–2464–2 (hardcover)
    1. Trials (Witchcraft)—Massachusetts—Salem—History—17th century—Juvenile
literature. 2. Witchcraft—Massachusetts—Salem—History—17th century—Juvenile
literature. [1. Trials (Witchcraft)—Massachusetts—Salem. 2. Witchcraft—Massachusetts—
Salem. 3. Salem (Mass.)—History—Colonial period, ca. 1600–1775.] I. Title. II. Series.
KFM2478.8.W5B67 2004
974.4'5—dc22   2003012552

Editorial Credits
Katy Kudela, editor; Kia Adams, series designer; Molly Nei, book designer and illustrator;
    Scott Thoms, photo researcher; Eric Kudalis, product planning editor

Photo Credits
Cover image: *Trial of George Jacobs*, by T. H. Matteson, Photo Courtesy Peabody Essex
Museum, 17290

Corbis/Bettmann, 6, 12, 15, 17, 30, 35; Lee Snider, 40
Courtesy of the Massachusetts Historical Society, 22
Getty Images/Hulton Archive, 29
Library of Congress, 36
North Wind Picture Archives, 5, 9, 10, 11, 23, 25, 26, 32, 39, 42, 43
Photo Courtesy Peabody Essex Museum, 17290, 20–21
Stock Montage Inc., 18, 19

1   2   3   4   5   6   09   08   07   06   05   04

Table of Contents

Chapter One

Witchcraft Casts Its Spell

In January 1692, two young girls in Salem Village, Massachusetts, began to behave strangely. Betty and Abigail screamed. They twisted their bodies into strange positions. Reverend Samuel Parris prayed for the girls to get better. But the girls did not get better. The village doctor examined the girls. The doctor told Parris that the girls were victims of witchcraft. The announcement spread fear through the village.

To make matters worse, both girls lived with Reverend Parris. Reverend Parris was the minister of Salem Village. He lived with his family and two slaves. Among the children were his daughter, 9-year-old Betty, and her cousin, 11-year-old Abigail Williams. Tituba, a woman from Barbados and the Parris' slave, helped care for the children.

Reverend Samuel Parris was terrified of witchcraft.
He hoped prayer would cure the girls.

Fear in Salem Village

Salem Village was located on the edge of a forest. Many of the villagers lived in fear of attacks from American Indians. This fear came from a war that ended 16 years earlier.

The Wampanoag Indians and colonists fought in a series of battles called King Philip's War (1675–1676). Troubles between the colonists and Wampanoag Indians had led to the war.

By 1692, **Puritans** feared that unfriendly American Indians still lived in the woods. Some of the girls among the "bewitched" had lost parents to attacks by American Indians. Ongoing fear of more attacks added to the stress of daily life. The combination of fear and stress may have caused the girls' strong emotional reactions. These reactions were thought of as acts of witchcraft.

Salem Village

During the 1600s, Salem Village was a poor farm community in the Massachusetts Bay **Colony**. The village was located outside of Salem Town. About 500 people lived in the village. At the center of the small village was a meetinghouse and a home for the minister.

Many villagers were Puritans. They had strict laws about church attendance, clothing, and other customs.

Life in Salem Village was hard. Sunday brought the only escape from endless work. Everyone was expected to attend church. Puritans attended both a morning and an afternoon service.

In 1692, Salem Village was the starting point of a witch hunt. Fear of witchcraft spread from Salem Village into Salem Town and throughout the colony. The Salem witch trials lasted four months. During this time, at least 150 people were arrested, 19 people were hanged, and one person was pressed to death. Several people also died in prison, but historians are not certain of the exact number.

Chapter Two

The Witch Hunt Begins

For thousands of years, people have used magic to explain things they do not understand. Beginning in the 1400s, most people in Europe believed witchcraft was the work of **Satan**. They thought Satan caused diseases and other bad events.

Settlers from Europe spread the belief in witchcraft to America. As did other groups, the Puritans of Salem Village feared witchcraft. Rumors spread throughout the village that Betty and Abigail were under a witch's spell. People from all around the village were curious. The two girls quickly became the center of attention.

Betty and Abigail began acting strangely in church. During prayers, the girls covered their ears and screamed.

A fear of witchcraft spread through Salem Village. Many Puritans thought prayer would help save the village.

Reverend Parris believed the only way to help the girls was to remove the witch from the village. Most people believed only the victims knew who was casting a spell on them. The girls would not tell anyone the name of the witch.

Cures for Witchcraft

People responded to witchcraft in several ways. Many people believed prayer would help cure

A group of young girls in Salem Village became known as "afflicted girls." These girls acted strangely. They claimed witches had put a spell on them.

Stories about Tituba

Many stories claim Tituba played a large role in the Salem witch trials. Many people believed Tituba told the girls about a type of religion called voodoo. People thought these stories put ideas into the girls' heads. But historians do not believe this theory. No evidence exists that Tituba practiced voodoo activities.

Court record of Tituba's statement

witchcraft. Reverend Parris spent his time praying. Meanwhile, Mary Sibley, a church member, asked Tituba to use magic to identify the witch. Both Mary and Tituba believed a special cake fed to the Parris' dog would identify the witch.

Before long, Ann Putnam and Elizabeth Hubbard began acting strangely. Six other girls also claimed to be victims of witchcraft. These girls, along with Betty and Abigail, became known throughout the area as the "afflicted girls."

Witches Named

Finally, Betty and Abigail named the first witch. They claimed Tituba practiced witchcraft. People easily believed she was a witch. She had proved she believed in witchcraft when she baked the cake for the Parris' dog. Tituba later confessed she had learned magic from a former employer who was a witch.

Claims of witchcraft terrified the people of Salem.

On February 25, 1692, Betty and Abigail accused Sarah Good and Sarah Osborne of witchcraft. The two women were unfriendly to others. It was not hard for the townspeople to imagine they were witches.

Charged with Witchcraft

Thomas Putnam was the father of young Ann. He brought charges against the accused witches, Sarah Good and Sarah Osborne. He went to the village leaders with Edward Putnam, Thomas Preston, and Joseph Hutchinson. Village leaders had to give their permission to arrest the accused women. Thomas Putnam filled out papers accusing the women of witchcraft.

Putnam's group arrested Sarah Good, Sarah Osborne, and Tituba on March 1, 1692. They took the women to the village meetinghouse. The judges held a hearing to hear the evidence. The charge was very serious. Witchcraft was punishable by death. The judges had to decide if the women should stand trial.

A large crowd gathered at the meetinghouse. Sarah Good and Sarah Osborne claimed innocence. Then, the afflicted girls began their strange behaviors. They claimed the women's specters were pinching and biting them. People believed a specter was a witch's spirit. Only the witch's victim could see the specter.

Tituba also claimed to be innocent. But she then changed her story. She admitted she was a witch. She said the other accused women were also witches. Tituba said that they had all flown on broomsticks. She added that she had seen other witches. She did not know their names. The judges believed all three women were witches. Sarah Good and Sarah Osborne were sent to jail to await trials.

Since Tituba confessed, the villagers believed she had broken Satan's hold. They thought she was no longer dangerous to the community. Tituba did not have to go to trial.

Witch Hunts in Europe

Witch-hunting peaked in Europe between 1580 and 1660. At least 100,000 people were executed in Europe on charges of witchcraft. The last witchcraft **execution** in Europe took place in Switzerland on June 17, 1782.

Trial by water was one method used to prove a witch's innocence or guilt. People believed a witch would float on the water. These "witches" were then hanged. Those people who sank in the water were declared innocent.

The trial by water method was used once in Hartford, Connecticut, during the 1660s. This form of testing ended before the Salem witch trials.

Chapter Three

Fear Spreads

By March 7, 1692, the accused witches were in jail. They awaited their trial. Yet, the girls continued to act strangely.

The villagers worried. The girls still seemed to be under a witch's spell. Tituba had said there were more witches in the village. Suddenly, neighbors began looking at each other with fear and distrust.

New Accusations

Thomas Putnam still led the witch hunt. His daughter claimed the specter of Martha Corey was hurting her. Martha was a respected member of the village. After several **accusations**, Martha was arrested.

Martha made it clear that she thought the girls were lying. She did not believe their claims.

People of all ages were accused of witchcraft and arrested during the Salem witch trials.

The Meetinghouse

The Puritans attended church services every Sunday. The services were held at the village meetinghouse. The meetinghouse was a plain, wooden building. In the winter, the villagers had no way to heat the building. They covered the windows with shutters, but the building was still cold. The shuttered windows also kept sunlight from lighting the meetinghouse. The minister read his sermons by candlelight. In 1692, the meetinghouse became the site of the witch-hunt trials.

During the hearing, the girls began howling.
The girls claimed Martha's specter was biting them.
They showed the judges bite marks on their arms.
Martha was taken to prison to await trial.
Next, the girls accused Rebecca Nurse.
Like Martha, Rebecca said the girls were telling lies.

Martha Corey was sent to prison. She was one of the first
to be accused of witchcraft.

The judges respected Rebecca. They decided to free her. Then the girls began screaming that Rebecca's specter was hurting them. The judges changed their minds and sent Rebecca to prison.

Many people believed Satan left his mark on witches. The people accused of witchcraft were questioned and searched. This 1853 painting by T. H. Matteson is titled *Examination of a Witch*.

More Accusations

Next, the girls accused Sarah Good's 4-year-old daughter. Little Dorcas Good was too young to understand what was happening. She

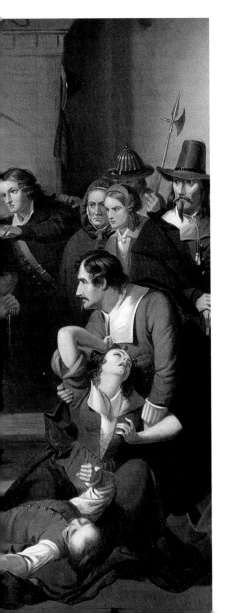

admitted that both she and her mother were witches. Dorcas was taken away in chains.

By late March, John Proctor had heard enough. His servant, Mary Warren, was one of the girls claiming to be under a witch's spell. He was angry. He believed the girls were causing trouble.

The girls immediately claimed they could see the specter of Proctor's wife, Elizabeth. When Proctor tried to defend his wife, the girls accused him of witchcraft. Both John and Elizabeth Proctor were arrested.

Court record of
Mary Warren's statement

Confession

The claims of witchcraft continued during the spring. The trials had not begun, but fear spread. People accused their enemies, neighbors, and family members of witchcraft.

By April, Mary Warren could no longer keep silent. She told the court that she and the other girls were faking their behavior. The other girls turned on Mary. They accused her of witchcraft. Mary was arrested and brought before the judges. Mary quickly changed her story. She said the girls were telling the truth. Mary was released from jail and never again spoke out against the other girls.

Statements made by the young girls brought fear to Salem Village. Soon, family and friends began to accuse one another of witchcraft.

Chapter Four

The Trials

On May 27, William Phipps, governor of the Massachusetts Bay Colony, formed an emergency court. The court was called the Court of Oyer and Terminer. Judges were told to reach quick, final decisions on each case. Phipps appointed a panel of seven judges. He then named William Stoughton as the chief judge.

The girls' behavior and their claims served as the main evidence. Cotton Mather, a leading Massachusetts minister, warned the panel. He wanted the judges to be careful about using specters as evidence. Mather was an expert on witchcraft. Mather believed Satan was tricking the girls into thinking they saw a witch's specter.

A panel of judges listened to people's statements. The judges then decided if the accused person was guilty or innocent of witchcraft.

The First Trial

The witch trials began June 2, 1692, with the trial of Bridget Bishop. Two men had accused her of sticking pins in rag dolls. This type of voodoo was practiced in the West Indies.

The trial did not go well for Bishop. When the girls gave their **testimony**, they thrashed about and shrieked. They claimed Bishop's specter was hurting them. The court found Bishop guilty. The judges sentenced her to hang at Gallows Hill near Salem.

Family members and friends feared the court's decision of guilt. People found guilty of witchcraft were sentenced to hang.

In Their Own Words

During the Salem witch trials, the court kept written records. Among these records are statements spoken by those men and women accused. "I am innocent of a witch," said Bridget Bishop during her trial.

Letters written during the witch trials are another source of information. In a letter to the judges, Mary Easty wrote before her death, " . . . if it be possible no more innocent blood be shed . . . I am clear of this **sin**."

Spectral Evidence

After Bishop's trial, the judges thought carefully about using spectral evidence. They wondered if Satan could take the form of an innocent person to trick the girls. Chief Justice William Stoughton insisted that spectral evidence be allowed. The girls could claim a witch's specter was biting or pinching them. The girls' claims would be enough evidence to charge a person with witchcraft.

Chapter Five

Guilty!

As the trials continued, it became clear that they were unfair. During Sarah Good's trial, a girl screamed that Good's specter was trying to stab her. Then the girl showed the court a broken knife blade. An observer stepped forward and said the blade was his. He had broken it earlier. The judges warned the girl not to lie again. But the judges continued to believe everything else she said. Good was charged as a witch. She was sentenced to die.

During Rebecca Nurse's trial, the court ruled that she was innocent. Suddenly, her accusers began howling that her specter was trying to kill them. A person in court claimed that one of the girls was sticking pins in her own knee. But the judges believed the girls.

The judges changed their decision to guilty.

People accused of witchcraft tried to defend themselves. The judges often did not believe them and announced decisions of guilt.

Spectral evidence continued to play the greatest role in the trials. The accuser's word was accepted without doubt. In most cases, there was no way to prove whether the girls were lying or telling the truth.

Bridget Bishop was taken to Gallows Hill and hanged.

Lord's Prayer

Puritans believed that a witch could not say the Lord's Prayer without stumbling over the words. Before his hanging, Reverend George Burroughs said the complete prayer, but he was hanged anyway.

The Executions

Bridget Bishop was the first person charged with witchcraft and sentenced to hang. On June 10, officials took Bishop from prison and loaded her into a cart. She was taken to Gallows Hill and hanged from a tree.

The second set of hangings took place on July 19. Five women, including Sarah Good and Rebecca Nurse, were hanged. Their dead bodies were cut down and tossed into a gap in the rocks on Gallows Hill.

On August 19, five more people were hanged. George Burroughs, once a minister in Salem Village, was put to death. John Proctor was also hanged. His wife, Elizabeth, was to be spared until after her baby was born.

The final hangings took place on September 22. Martha Corey and seven other people were hanged at Gallows Hill.

Unusual Death

Giles Corey also met his death in September. During his hearing, he pleaded not guilty. But Corey refused to be part of the trial. According to law, a person who refused to stand for trial was

Giles Corey memorial stone

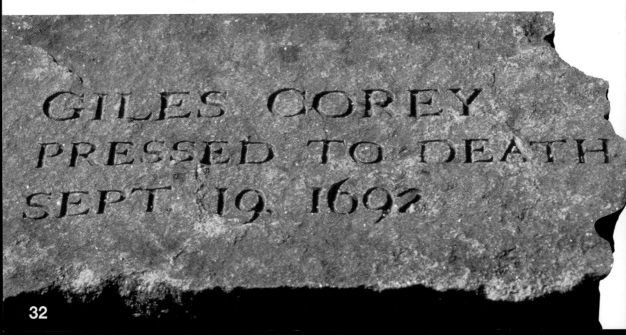

sentenced to death. Corey was placed on his back in a nearby field with a board on his chest. Heavy rocks were piled on top, slowly crushing him to death. This was the only time this form of punishment was used in the colony.

Salem Village, 1692

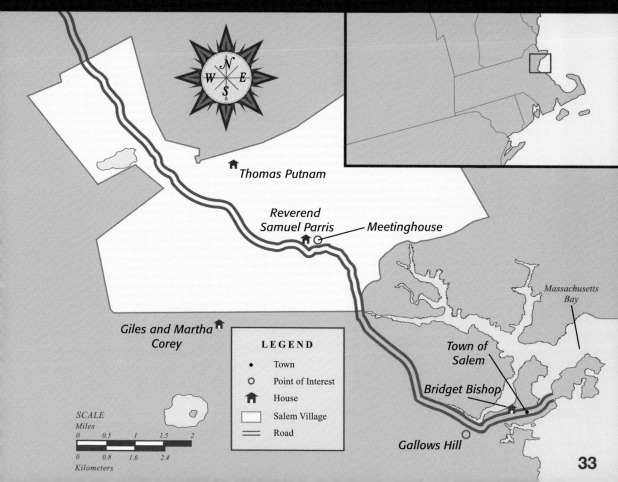

Thomas Putnam

Reverend Samuel Parris — Meetinghouse

Massachusetts Bay

Giles and Martha Corey

LEGEND

● Town
○ Point of Interest
🏠 House
▢ Salem Village
= Road

Town of Salem

Bridget Bishop

Gallows Hill

SCALE
Miles
0   0.5   1   1.5   2

0   0.8   1.6   2.4
Kilometers

Chapter Six

Sanity Returns

By the fall of 1692, nearly every family in the Salem area had been touched in some way by the witch hunt. Twenty people had been killed because of witchcraft charges. As many as 350 more people were accused of witchcraft.

Public opinion was starting to change. People were beginning to doubt the girls. Some believed Satan was tricking the girls. Others thought the girls were lying on purpose.

The girls began accusing some of Massachusetts' richest and most powerful people. After the girls accused the wife of Governor Phipps, he began to stop the witch hunts. On October 11, Governor Phipps ended the arrests for witchcraft. By the end of October, he closed the court that heard the cases.

By fall, many began to doubt the girls' statements. This drawing by Howard Pyle shows a court scene during the Salem witch trials.

A new court heard the remaining cases. Spectral evidence was not allowed. In January 1693, the remaining cases were heard. At least 50 people were accused. Only three people were found guilty and sentenced to death. Governor Phipps later took back their death sentences and set them free.

Governor William Phipps ordered that the Salem witch trials be stopped. In May 1693, he dropped the charges of those people still in prison on the charge of witchcraft.

Destroyed Lives

Nineteen people had been hanged for witchcraft during the Salem witch trials. One man had been killed for not agreeing to take part in the court process. Other people, including Sarah Osborne, died while in prison.

Most of the accused survived the witch hunt, but they had suffered. Before they could be released from prison, they had to pay a jailer's fee. This fee paid for fuel, clothing, food, legal paperwork, and court costs.

Many families lost everything they owned during the witch hunt. When a person was found guilty, the person charged lost the right to own possessions. The sheriff took all farm animals and household goods. Even if the accused were cleared of charges, it was not easy for them to rebuild their lives. Many villagers continued to believe the accused really were witches.

Changing the Records

The freed prisoners asked two things of the government. They wanted their records wiped clean of witchcraft charges. They also wanted their belongings returned.

In 1710, the government of the Massachusetts Bay Colony reversed the charges of the people who died as a result of the witch hunt. The government also made payments to 24 families. These families had lost family members or property during the witch hunt.

Some people tried to make up for their part in the witch trials. Judge Samuel Sewall apologized for his role. Tituba took back her whole story. She confessed that Reverend Parris forced her to lie. In 1706, Ann Putnam confessed in church. She said none of the stories had been true. She claimed Satan had tricked her.

Beyond the Salem Witch Trials

The girls who were responsible for the tragedy in Salem Village were never punished. Their actions harmed many, but they were not held responsible.

Samuel Sewall
apologized for his role in
the Salem witch trials.
He had served as a judge
on the Court of Oyer
and Terminer.

The Salem witch trials changed the lives of the villagers. Even the American court system changed. The Salem witch trials were the last time spectral evidence was ever allowed in trials.

IN MEMORY OF THOSE INNOCENTS
WHO DIED DURING THE
SALEM VILLAGE WITCHCRAFT HYSTERIA
OF 1692

In 1992, a memorial was completed in memory of those who died during the Salem witch trials. The memorial stands in Danvers, Massachusetts.

Witch Hunts in U.S. History

In 1953, Arthur Miller's play *The Crucible* appeared on Broadway. The play was based on the 1692 Salem witch trials.

Miller added his own ideas in the play. The subject of the play was the McCarthy hearings that took place in the 1950s.

During the 1950s, Senator Joseph McCarthy led a committee that accused people of belonging to the Communist Party. **Communism** was the government system of the former Soviet Union. At the time, the United States and the Soviet Union did not have good relations. McCarthy thought people who believed in communism were enemies of the United States. The committee often had little evidence against the people it accused. The McCarthy hearings ruined many people's careers.

Today, Salem Village is known as Danvers, Massachusetts. Many years have passed, but the Salem witch trials are remembered. A memorial stands in Danvers. This memorial was built in memory of those who died during the witch trials.

Time Line

Sarah Good and Sarah Osborne plead innocent of witchcraft, but Tituba pleads guilty; the women are sent to jail to await trial.

Betty Parris and Abigail Williams begin acting strangely.

Bridget Bishop is hanged on Gallows Hill; her death is the first of the Salem witch trials.

January 1692 February 1692 March 1692 May 1692 June 1692

Sarah Good, Sarah Osborne, and Tituba are named as witches.

William Phipps, governor of the Massachusetts Bay Colony, appoints an emergency court of judges; this court is called the Court of Oyer and Terminer.

On September 19,
Giles Corey is
pressed to death.

Governor Phipps drops
the charges for everyone
still in prison on the
charge of witchcraft.

Five more people are
hanged on Gallows Hill
as convicted witches.

| July 1692 | August 1692 | September 1692 | October 1692 | May 1693 |

Five women are hanged on
Gallows Hill as witches.

Governor
Phipps stops
the witch trials
in Salem.

On September 22, eight
people are hanged on
Gallows Hill.

Glossary

accusation (ak-yoo-ZAY-shuhn)—a charge of wrongdoing

colony (KOL-uh-nee)—a territory that has been settled by people from another country

communism (KOM-yuh-niz-uhm)—a way of organizing a country so that all the land, houses, and factories belong to the government and the profits are shared by all

execution (ek-suh-KYOO-shuhn)—being put to death as punishment for a crime

Puritan (PYOOR-uh-tuhn)—a member of a group of Protestants in the 16th and 17th centuries who followed a strict moral code

Satan (SAY-tuhn)—the devil or an evil spirit

sin (SIN)—bad or evil behavior that goes against moral or religious laws

testimony (TESS-tuh-moh-nee)—a statement given by a witness in a court of law

Read More

Asirvatham, Sandy. *The Salem Witch Trials.* Great Disasters, Reforms and Ramifications. Philadelphia: Chelsea House, 2002.

Dolan, Edward F. *The Salem Witch Trials.* Kaleidoscope. New York: Benchmark Books/Marshall Cavendish, 2002.

Kallen, Stuart A. *The Salem Witch Trials.* The World History Series. San Diego: Lucent Books, 1999.

MacBain, Jenny. *The Salem Witch Trials: A Primary Source History of the Witchcraft Trials in Salem, Massachusetts.* Primary Sources in American History. New York: Rosen, 2003.

Wilson, Lori Lee. *The Salem Witch Trials.* How History Is Invented. Minneapolis: Lerner, 1997.

Useful Addresses

John Ward House
East India Square
Salem, MA 01970
Visitors to this museum tour will learn about life during the Salem witch trials. The John Ward house was built in Salem in 1684.

**Salem Village
Witchcraft Memorial**
176 Hobart Street
Danvers, MA 01923
This memorial honors all of the 1692 witchcraft trial victims; it is located across the street from where the original Salem Village meetinghouse stood.

Salem Witch Museum
Washington Square
Salem, MA 01970
This Salem museum uses stage sets with life-size figures to give a brief history of the Salem witch trials of 1692.

Salem Witch Trials Memorial
Liberty Street
Salem, MA 01970
This memorial was dedicated in 1992 to the victims of the Salem witch trials of 1692.

Internet Sites

FactHound offers a safe, fun way to find Internet sites related to this book. All of the sites on FactHound have been researched by our staff.

Here's how:
1. Visit *www.facthound.com*
2. Type in this special code **0736824642** for age-appropriate sites.
   Or enter a search word related to this book for a more general search.
3. Click on the Fetch It button.

FactHound will fetch the best sites for you!

Index